Every Day
She Rose

Every Day She Rose

by Andrea Scott
and Nick Green

Playwrights Canada Press

Toronto

For professional or amateur production rights, please contact:
Colin Rivers at Marquis Entertainment
PO Box 47026, Eaton Centre, Toronto, ON M5B 2P9
416-960-9123 x 223 | info@mqlit.ca

LIBRARY AND ARCHIVES CANADA CATALOGUING IN PUBLICATION
Title: Every day she rose / by Andrea Scott & Nick Green.
Names: Scott, Andrea, 1971- (Playwright), author. | Green, Nick (Playwright), author.
Description: A play.
Identifiers: Canadiana (print) 20220209340 | Canadiana (ebook) 20220209383
    | ISBN 9780369103383 (softcover) | ISBN 9780369103390 (PDF)
    | ISBN 9780369103406 (HTML)
Classification: LCC PS8637.C675 E94 2022 | DDC C812/.6—dc23

Playwrights Canada Press operates on land which is the ancestral home of the Anishinaabe Nations (Ojibwe / Chippewa, Odawa, Potawatomi, Algonquin, Saulteaux, Nipissing, and Mississauga), the Wendat, and the members of the Haudenosaunee Confederacy (Mohawk, Oneida, Onondaga, Cayuga, Seneca, and Tuscarora), as well as Metis and Inuit peoples. It always was and always will be Indigenous land.

We acknowledge the support of the Canada Council for the Arts, the Ontario Arts Council (OAC), Ontario Creates, and the Government of Canada for our publishing activities.

Canada Council   Conseil des arts
for the Arts   du Canada

ONTARIO ARTS COUNCIL
CONSEIL DES ARTS DE L'ONTARIO
an Ontario government agency
un organisme du gouvernement de l'Ontario

Canada

ONTARIO | ONTARIO
CREATES | CRÉATIF

This is for all the Black and Brown women, persisting, enduring, and thriving.

—Andrea

Every Day She Rose was first produced by Nightwood Theatre at Buddies in Bad Times Theatre, Toronto, from November 24 to December 8, 2019, with the following cast and creative team:

Starring: Monice Peter and Adrian Shepherd-Gawinski

Directors: Sedina Fiati and Andrea Donaldson
Stage Manager: Lucy McPhee
Sound Design: Cosette Pin
Set Design: Michelle Tracey
Costume Design: Ming Wong
Lighting Design: Rebecca Picherack
Production Manager: Pip Bradford

Characters

Mark
Cathy-Ann
Nick
Andrea

Scene 1

July 3, 2016. In the condo, around 1 p.m. Pride will be starting soon, and MARK *is standing beside the door dressed in shorts and a tank top. He's impatient.* CATHY-ANN, *dressed like a sentient rainbow, is running around half-dressed, finding a hat, fixing her makeup, etc.*

MARK: Cathy-Ann, will you please hurry the fucking fuck up?

CATHY-ANN: I'm hurrying!

MARK: I want to get a good spot.

CATHY-ANN: We have lots of time.

Do you have bottles of water?

MARK: I put them in your purse.

CATHY-ANN: Okay. I guess I'm bringing a purse.

MARK: I'll carry it. Are you stressing?

CATHY-ANN: No.

MARK: Don't stress, girl.

CATHY-ANN: I'm not . . . girl.

MARK: All right. Let's go.

CATHY-ANN: Mark, I need five more minutes.

MARK: Oh my Godddddddd!

CATHY-ANN: I don't understand why you're suddenly in such a rush. You were lying on the couch until three minutes ago.

MARK: My back was hurting. From the sex. It was very vigorous.

CATHY-ANN: I could hear.

MARK: I was trying to keep him quiet.

CATHY-ANN: And he was . . . ?

MARK: Steven.

CATHY-ANN: I'm sure he's very nice.

MARK: Yeah, I guess.

CATHY-ANN: How long have you known this one?

MARK: Since *(looks at watch)* 11:47 p.m. last night. When he arrived.

CATHY-ANN: *(cooly)* Cool.

MARK: You know, if you spent less time judging me, we'd probably get to the parade faster.

CATHY-ANN: I'm not judging you.

MARK: Oh no. *Cool.*

CATHY-ANN: I just don't love the whole *having strangers in my home thing.*

MARK: I wouldn't invite anyone over if I thought they were unstable or something.

CATHY-ANN: You talk to them on your app for like half an hour.

MARK: I have a very intense screening process.

CATHY-ANN: Oh, do you?

MARK: Yeah. It goes like this: "Wassup? You crazy? Great, come over."

CATHY-ANN: Wow.

MARK: Wow?

CATHY-ANN: Have you ever thought that maybe you're reading judgment in me because you're judging yourself? It's called projection.

MARK: All right. Calm down, Oprah. Can we go now? I want to get a good spot.

CATHY-ANN: You're a hundred feet tall. You can see from anywhere.

MARK: I want a spot where I can get close to my husband.

CATHY-ANN: Your husband?

MARK: Justin.

CATHY-ANN looks confused.

TRUDEAU! We have a connection. He'll know it as soon as we lock eyes. Sorry, Sophie.

CATHY-ANN: Right. I forgot that you've found politics now.

MARK: I've always been political. Oh, you look cute in those shorts.

CATHY-ANN: Right?

MARK: Like so fucking pretty. Your legs are so killer.

CATHY-ANN: Thanks! It's the wedges.

MARK: Honestly, how are you single?

CATHY-ANN: My standards are too high?

MARK: If you get hit on more than I do . . .

CATHY-ANN: I somehow doubt that this will be where I meet the man of my dreams.

MARK: You already have.

CATHY-ANN: Let's not start on how problematic that is.

MARK: Oooooh. "Problematic."

CATHY-ANN rolls her eyes and picks up her purse. It weighs a ton.

CATHY-ANN: God. It's like a suitcase. What's in here?

MARK: Just the essentials. For both of us.

She pulls out a large bottle of sunscreen.

You can use it too. It's SPF 75.

CATHY-ANN: Overkill, love.

MARK: Hey, I don't hear you complaining about the sandwiches I made us. With my own hands!

CATHY-ANN: No mayo?

MARK: I know you hate white creamy sauces.

CATHY-ANN: 'Kay. But you have to carry it part of the time.

MARK: I said that I would carry it. Are you gonna be pissy like this all day?

CATHY-ANN: I'm not being pissy.

MARK: You are. You've been like this since you woke up.

CATHY-ANN: Woke up? That implies that I got some sleep during fuck-a-palooza last night. Jesus. Talkin' about white creamy sauces . . .

MARK: It's Pride. It's supposed to be, like, a party time.

CATHY-ANN: I know.

MARK: And I mean, it's my place—

CATHY-ANN throws her hands up in exasperation.

—too. I was going to say it's my place, too.

CATHY-ANN: Right.

MARK: Cathy-Ann, come on. Let's not get all bitchy bitchy with each other, biiiiiitch. I just wanna have fun. I wanna have fun with my bestie. With my queen. My Goddess.

CATHY-ANN cracks a smile.

There we go. Can we have fun? Get a little drank? Throw some shade and drink some tea, bitch?

CATHY-ANN: *(smiling)* Don't call me bitch.

MARK: Okay, bitch. I won't, bitch. I promise. Bitch.

CATHY-ANN: I'm gonna smack you.

MARK: Smack my dick. Are you ready?

CATHY-ANN: As I'm going to be.

MARK: Then let's motherfucking go!!!

CATHY-ANN crosses to the door, opens it, and as she exits, turns and tosses her purse to MARK, who catches it.

Fuck, this is heavy.

(as he exits) Can't you just carry it first?

Scene 2

CATHY-ANN and MARK are standing on opposite sides of the stage. They speak directly to the audience, not speaking in relation to each other.

MARK: I wanted to stand up by Wellesley.

CATHY-ANN: It was too crowded up north on Yonge.

MARK: Cathy-Ann said it was too crowded.

CATHY-ANN: Also down by Dundas Square.

MARK: She didn't want to stand near Dundas Square either.

CATHY-ANN: Too many people!

MARK: Part of me was like, *are you going to be like this all day?*

CATHY-ANN: He was definitely starting to turn on the attitude.

MARK: But then I was also a little like . . . if anything like Orlando was going to *happen* . . . it would be either near Dundas Square or Wellesley.

CATHY-ANN: It was hot. I just wanted some shade.

MARK: So we end up just north of Gerrard. It's like . . . straightsville down there.

CATHY-ANN: He called it *straightsville*, and I was like . . . and your point is?

MARK: Straights and lezzies. But I didn't say lezzie.

CATHY-ANN: Anyways, I thought our spot was good.

MARK: It wasn't a bad spot. Not great, but whatever. If we'd just been a bit *earlier*. But whatever.

CATHY-ANN: The parade had just started when we arrived. There was a huge swell of energy.

MARK: I love the beginning. There's this roar that travels down the street, cheers and the dykes on bikes.

CATHY-ANN: It's pretty amazing when it starts.

MARK: Cheering.

CATHY-ANN: Laughing.

MARK: Beads.

CATHY-ANN: Water guns. Don't get my hair WET!

MARK: Get me WET!

CATHY-ANN: It gets louder and louder and hyper and crazy!

MARK: It gets hotter and hotter.

CATHY-ANN: We wave and scream.

MARK: We wave and laugh and scream.

CATHY-ANN: And dance.

MARK: It's hilarious.

CATHY-ANN: I could feel a blister starting.

MARK: It's happiness. Total happiness.

CATHY-ANN: And that's just the first half-hour.

MARK: And thennnn . . .

CATHY-ANN: Just two more hours to go.

MARK: I'm always like . . . oh that was just the beginning.

CATHY-ANN: The TD Bank float goes by.

MARK: Hot guys in green speedos.

CATHY-ANN: Then RBC.

MARK: Hot guys in blue speedos.

CATHY-ANN: Then "You're Richer Than You Think."

MARK: Red speedos?

CATHY-ANN: More water guns.

MARK: Okaaayyyy, enough with the water guns.

CATHY-ANN: Then the cops.

MARK: Spray them. Spray *them*!

CATHY-ANN: There are lots of them.

MARK: It's always great to see the cops just relax. They're, like, laughing, wearing beads, shaking hands, and hugging people.

CATHY-ANN: I always think it's weird the way the cops are here versus at other events. It's like they're partying here. Like they aren't even worried about anything

MARK: I'm glad to see them today. After Orlando, it makes me wonder a little bit about who else is around us, watching.

CATHY-ANN: Like are they just here because they have to be?

MARK: I'm suddenly aware of who's around me. Like . . . is there, like, what are they called? csis? Is that what they're called? Like do you think csis is here now?

CATHY-ANN: I know I shouldn't, but I think some of these cops are really hot.

MARK: But also, like, who else is around me? Like are there any whackos with like backpacks or hands in their coat, or whatever. Like maybe I shouldn't have come here. Maybe we should have just gone to Hanlan's.

CATHY-ANN: Suddenly the cheers get really loud up the street.

MARK: A giant swarm of people. Spectators crowding close.

CATHY-ANN: Geez. Stop pushing already.

MARK: There's a flock of people in front of me. Move! Get the fuck out of the way!

CATHY-ANN: I get my elbows out.

MARK: They think they're gonna get in front of me, but they forgot.

CATHY-ANN: Thank God for Mark.

MARK: I am the Ganglezar.

CATHY-ANN: He is the Ganglezar.

MARK: It's a matter of starting with your hands like a wedge. Then you do the breaststroke. And voila. Front-row seats.

CATHY-ANN: I have to hand it to him—it works.

MARK & CATHY-ANN: Ganglezar strikes again.

MARK: And just in the nick of time. As we take possession of our now-perfect front-row spot.

CATHY-ANN: There he is.

MARK: The first prime minister to walk in Pride.

CATHY-ANN: Justin Trudeau. In pink.

MARK: A glorious salmon shirt.

CATHY-ANN: Damn that is one handsome man.

MARK: And he's *wet*.

CATHY-ANN: Kathleen Wynne is there with him, too.

MARK: The mayor's there. What's his . . . Tory? Mayor Tory. And I'm like . . . you like the gays, Mayor Tory?

CATHY-ANN: All three levels walking together. That's a pretty amazing sight to see.

MARK: JUSTIN! JUSTIN, I'M OVER . . . I LOVE YOU, JUSTIN, LOOK AT ME!!!

CATHY-ANN: Mark starts losing it.

MARK: I start to lose it.

CATHY-ANN: Justin keeps walking.

MARK: He keeps on walking.

CATHY-ANN: Mark's still losing it.

MARK: I'm still losing it. I'm screaming "JUSTIN! JUSTIN!" But he doesn't hear me.

CATHY-ANN: A man walking behind him gives us a look. It feels like a warning.

MARK: JUSTIN!

CATHY-ANN: I put my hand on Mark to calm him down.

MARK: I'm like . . . what?

CATHY-ANN: I don't like the look that man is giving us.

MARK: Cathy-Ann's making a stink face about something.

CATHY-ANN: He finally calms down.

MARK: Like I was just excited. Like *everyone* is screaming. But whatever.

CATHY-ANN: The guy moves on with the rest of the parade.

MARK: And Justin is gone. Just like my chances of being first lady of Canada. Thanks a lot, Cathy-Ann.

CATHY-ANN: I really didn't like the look on that guy's face.

MARK: I'm starting to feel like dancing. It's probably because I've switched to vodka Fresca.

CATHY-ANN: I just want to stick it out until PFLAG.

MARK: I have to pee.

CATHY-ANN: This blister is screaming at me.

MARK: Suddenly the parade just kind of . . . stops.

CATHY-ANN: Everyone's looking up the street.

MARK: There's something happening a couple blocks up.

CATHY-ANN: People start heading up the block to see what's going on.

MARK: I'm like . . . uh, I don't like this.

CATHY-ANN: I start going with the crowd, dragging Mark behind me.

MARK: I'm thinking maybe we should just go.

CATHY-ANN: We arrive at Yonge and College and see a bunch of people dressed in black.

MARK: What the fuck?

CATHY-ANN: A bunch of Black people dressed in black.

MARK: Some Black woman with a bullhorn.

CATHY-ANN: It's Black Lives Matter.

MARK: Other people in black start sitting down.

CATHY-ANN: They've stopped the parade.

MARK: She's stopped our parade.

CATHY-ANN: Black Lives Matter has stopped the parade.

Switch.

ANDREA: Sorry, no. I have a—sorry, Nick.

NICK: It's okay.

ANDREA: It's the part where I say . . . um . . . I say *a bunch of people dressed in black*, then I say *a bunch of Black people dressed in black.*

NICK: Yeah.

ANDREA: I know what you're doing with that, it's poetic and has a nice rhythm.

NICK: Yeah, I think it has the one-two build thing that I like.

ANDREA: I know, but I don't think I would say *a bunch of people* and then *a bunch of Black people.* I think I would say—sorry, Cathy-Ann the character would say *a bunch of people.* I wouldn't reference race. People mention race to delineate otherness and since Cathy-Ann is Black, she just sees people.

NICK: Right.

ANDREA: Unless she can't see that they're Black right away. Can she not see?

NICK: I don't know. It could be.

ANDREA: Okay, good. What did you think about my part about the cops?

NICK: It's great. I love the rewrite.

ANDREA: Was it too on the nose?

NICK: Not at all. I think he should love the police even more.

ANDREA: I don't know. I'm not sure that Mark necessarily has to, like, *love* the police.

NICK: It's more conflict, isn't it? And there's the whole post-Orlando part.

ANDREA: I know, but he's so tone deaf. I don't want people to hate him. To him the police are like background noise, so he's indifferent.

NICK: This is pre-Bruce McArthur, don't forget.

ANDREA: Right. Right, yeah, that's true.

NICK: For a gay of his young age.

ANDREA: How old is he? Are we still thinking twenty-eight?

NICK: Yeah. Like twenty-nine? Not quite thirty but feeling like a big adult because he owns a condo. Does that feel right for Cathy-Ann?

ANDREA: I like twenty-nine for her too because it adds a level of reality to the fact that she has like two degrees and still works temp jobs.

NICK: She has two degrees now? That's impressive.

ANDREA: I think she just finished her masters in psych, and before that she majored in something like . . .

NICK: Equity studies.

ANDREA: No, I mean like anthropology or something.

NICK: Totally. I think that Mark has to be played by a gay actor. I want him to *sound* gay.

ANDREA: Are you casting the play before it's even finished?

NICK: I'm just saying. And he needs to be tall. And should probably be handsome and naturally charming . . .

ANDREA: Mhmm . . .

NICK: *(strikes a pose)* Now where might we find an actor like that?

ANDREA: Nick, aren't you almost forty?

NICK: Please! I am a dewy thirty-five years old. And seventeen months. But there's always Botox!

ANDREA: So Scene 3?

NICK: Yes! Okay, so Scene 3, which is also the start of the second act given that we just had our inciting incident. The status quo has now shifted forever and now they're back home and it's like 10 p.m. They're supposed to go out partying that night but something is . . . off.

ANDREA: Right, so . . . Cathy-Ann is sitting on the couch and you're off:

Scene 3

July 2016. It's 10 p.m. the night of the parade. CATHY-ANN *is reading in the living room.*

Music blasts as MARK *walks out of his bedroom in nothing but a T-shirt and his underwear, carrying an empty cocktail glass and talking on the phone.*

MARK: *(on the phone)* What a slut. No, seriously, what a fucking slut. How long did they even know each other, like a minute? Well no, I mean I know they knew each other from before, obviously, he was dating Cameron. Yeah he was. Yeah he was. Okay not dating but whatever. Fucking. Exactly. So don't you think it's kinda shady that now they're banging?

He has walked over to the booze and is about to mix himself a drink. He tries to get CATHY-ANN's *attention, but she is engrossed in her book. He whispers, trying not to let on to the guy on the phone that he's not listening:*

Cathy-Ann. Pssst. Bitch. Biiiiitch. Lady. Lady biiiiitch. Lady bitch!

CATHY-ANN *is startled and looks over. He gestures "drink?" and she shakes her head no.*

(to the guy on the phone) Yeah totally.

MARK *gestures to* CATHY-ANN *"oh yes you will" about having a drink. She shakes her head no again. He vigorously mimes that she is going to take a drink and get drunk. She keeps shaking her*

head and he keeps miming back. It gets frantic and over the top, then suddenly:

(to the guy on the phone) Sorry, what? Oh. Shorts and a tank top. Yeeeeah. What about you?

MARK pours two drinks and brings one over to CATHY-ANN. He sits down on the couch next to her.

(to the guy on the phone) That sounds cute. With the black Nikes? Hot. No, it's so cute. No, not cute like femme cute, cute like track-and-field cute. I know. I want to get one of those pairs of shorts with like the slits up the side. You do?!?! Can I borrow? Wait no you're like tiny. No, they won't, I have child-bearing hips. No, I wouldn't be able to get those up one thigh. Baby got back, Becky. Yes you are. You're Becky. Do you have good hair? Then you're fucking Becky. Shut up. You wish. Anyways. What time are you going? We're going to Uber. Well yeah, I'm not fucking taking transit. What, are you? Obviously. So I'll see you in like half an hour then. Okay good. But we didn't have this conversation. Seriously, girl. Girl. Seriously, okay? Good. Bye, girl, bye.

He hangs up and flops back on the couch.

I fucking hate Andrew right now. He's making me fucking crazy. Anyways. This is your forty-five-minute call.

CATHY-ANN: Didn't you just say you'd be there in half an hour?

MARK: Bussssssted. I lied. Cheers. You're gonna leave me hanging in this cheers? Catttthy-Annnnn. Come on. Come on and cheers me. Commmmme onnnnnn!

CATHY-ANN rolls her eyes and cheers him.

Good girl. Now get ready. I'm gonna pump the T Swift.

CATHY-ANN: That parade was really intense. Everyone's posting about it.

MARK: *(checking his phone)* Yeah, so weird.

CATHY-ANN: You haven't really said much about it.

MARK: What's to say?

CATHY-ANN: Something more than "*so weird*"? That's all you'd say on the way home.

MARK: Well it was.

CATHY-ANN: Remember this thing we used to do called *having a conversation*?

MARK: Yes. But I also remember this thing called *getting wastey*. Let's do that instead.

CATHY-ANN: I'm not feeling it.

Beat. CATHY-ANN *goes back to reading.* MARK *sighs and
sits down.*

MARK: Okay. I guess what I mean by *so weird* is that it was like so
tense. Which for Pride is like . . . so weird.

CATHY-ANN: Yeah. They were not fucking around.

MARK: I thought everyone was gonna be sent home or something like
a bomb threat.

CATHY-ANN: To be honest, at first I was kind of pissed off. Because it's
your day.

MARK: Ohmigod! Me too! Like what the fuck? Now?? You gotta do
this NOW?

CATHY-ANN: But then I was like "whoa!" They have serious demands.

MARK: Yeah . . .

CATHY-ANN: I'm reading all this stuff now about it, police and the
Black queer community, the violence against Black trans people. I
mean, I can see what they were fighting for.

MARK: Sure.

CATHY-ANN: To be Black and trans and queer . . . it must be enraging,
fucking triggering to see the police at the parade when they've been a
target for so long.

MARK: But to be saying that there shouldn't be any cops there? Even
after?

CATHY-ANN: Even after . . .

MARK: Orlando. A whole shit ton of gay guys were like *just* shot dead in a gay bar.

CATHY-ANN: And most of them were Latinx.

MARK: So? What does that have to do with them being murdered?

CATHY-ANN: It was Latin night and the shooter knew that.

MARK: How do you know that he knew that?

CATHY-ANN: It's common knowledge.

MARK: Okay, but he still killed them all because they're gay.

CATHY-ANN: I keep hearing people say that. You can't just erase who they are to co-opt their tragedy.

MARK: I'm not trying to co-opt their tragedy! I'm just a little busy being fucking terrified that some homophobe's gonna show up and kill me while I'm dancing or something.

CATHY-ANN: And for some queer people of colour, that homophobe could have a badge and a gun.

MARK: So no cops at a gay celebration.

CATHY-ANN: No. No no no no no. No cops in *uniform* marching in the parade.

MARK: I don't get that. I'm sorry, but I don't. And I don't think stopping the celebration was the best way to try to get that message across. Coming to our parade—

CATHY-ANN: Our? They were the guests of honour. The majority of BLM are LGBTQ.

MARK: And now I know my ABCs. Been doing some googling?

CATHY-ANN: Yes. You should too.

MARK: I'm good. I want police there. It's a matter of safety.

CATHY-ANN: For white people.

MARK: Okay. Fine. I don't have the right to feel safe?

CATHY-ANN: No, of course you do. But don't I?

MARK: Well you don't see me stopping Caribana, do you?

CATHY-ANN: No, Mark, you'd have to actually *go* to Caribana for that to happen.

Switch.

NICK: Okay, I think we need to talk this moment out.

ANDREA: I agree.

NICK: This is the most pivotal moment in the show.

ANDREA: I think this is one of them.

NICK: I mean, this is it, this is where the conflict lies. The fundamental moment where they just can't see eye to eye.

ANDREA: *Won't.* Where Mark won't even try to see any other perspective. Here, let's try this:

Switch.

MARK: Well you don't see me sitting down at Caribana.

CATHY-ANN: No, Mark, you have to actually go to Caribana in order to do that.

MARK: I'd rather not get shot, thank you very much.

Switch.

ANDREA: See, it's the racism.

NICK: Mhmm . . .

Switch.

MARK: Well you don't see me sitting down at Caribana.

CATHY-ANN: No, Mark, you have to actually go to Caribana in order to do that.

MARK: I'd rather not get beaten up, thank you so much.

Switch.

NICK: It's only a little change, but I think it's a bit more fair.

ANDREA: More fair?

NICK: Not more fair. I mean more accurate. Like, I don't think gays like Mark—and I'm not saying like *me*—like Mark, I'm not so sure they'd worry about getting shot so much as beaten up for being gay.

ANDREA: Ugh, that's so ignorant.

NICK: Mark's a bit of a dumdum when he's mad, I think.

Switch.

MARK: Well you don't see me sitting down at Caribana.

CATHY-ANN: No, Mark, you would actually have to go to Caribana in order to do that.

MARK: I'd rather not get beaten up, thank you so much.

CATHY-ANN: Why would you get beaten up?

MARK: Um, because Jamaican's are homophobic?

CATHY-ANN: Funny. I'm not homophobic . . .

MARK: You're also not "Jamaican."

CATHY-ANN: Really.

Switch.

ANDREA: I don't think that's going anywhere.

Switch.

MARK: You don't see me sitting down at Caribana.

CATHY-ANN: Listen up, you Taylor Swift worshipping, glitter wearing, vodka slurping, ignorant, racist motherfucker—

Switch.

NICK: Whoa whoa whoa! That's a very different Cathy-Ann than what we're writing.

ANDREA: Sorry, I just wanted to get it out of my system.

NICK: How'd it feel?

ANDREA: Fucking great.

NICK: Get it, girl.

ANDREA: Yeah.

NICK: Sorry, I don't know why I just did that.

Switch.

MARK: You don't see me sitting down at Caribana.

CATHY-ANN: No, Mark, you would actually have to go to Caribana in order to do that.

MARK: You know, Black people aren't the only people who are oppressed.

CATHY-ANN: Yes, please keep reminding me of that as you work your way up the corporate ladder—

MARK: What was the point of them stopping the parade? Not enough inclusion of Black people in Pride, right?

CATHY-ANN: No, yes and no, the police—

MARK: What inclusion has there been for gay people at Caribana?

Switch.

NICK: What inclusion *has* there been for gay people at Caribana?

ANDREA: Have you ever actually been to Caribana?

NICK: Me? Yes. Once.

ANDREA: Yeah.

Switch.

MARK: What inclusion has there been for gay people at Caribana?

CATHY-ANN: That's not a fair comparison.

MARK: Why not?

CATHY-ANN: It just isn't.

MARK: Oh, great argument. *It just isn't.*

CATHY-ANN: What happened today—

MARK: What happened today?

CATHY-ANN: What happened today changed everything.

MARK: Oh, did it?

CATHY-ANN: Yes.

MARK: And what, exactly, did it change? Other than making the parade even longer than the unbearable length that it already is?

CATHY-ANN: Forget it.

MARK: What did it change?

Switch.

ANDREA: I don't think she knows yet.

NICK: But what did it change?

ANDREA: Police at Pride. The management of the event. The visibility of racial issues in the Village. Relationships, friendships . . .

NICK: But for Cathy-Ann, what did it change?

Switch.

MARK: What did it change, Cathy-Ann?

CATHY-ANN: Us. You and me. Mainly me.

MARK: Whatever.

Switch.

ANDREA: Go again.

Switch.

MARK: You don't see me sitting down at Caribana.

CATHY-ANN: No, Mark, you'd have to actually go to Caribana in order for that to happen.

MARK: Whatever.

Switch.

NICK: That's it? He just says whatever?

ANDREA: Shuts the whole conversation down.

NICK: I like it.

Switch.

MARK: Whatever, Cathy-Ann.

CATHY-ANN: Huh. Well . . . I just . . . the idea of hitting the Village feels kind of wrong to me now.

MARK: What?

CATHY-ANN: I don't feel comfortable going tonight—I'm going to stay in.

MARK: No, you're not.

CATHY-ANN: Yeah, I think I should.

MARK: No. You're not.

CATHY-ANN: Yes. I am.

MARK: You're bailing on me now? What the fuck?

CATHY-ANN: You have, like, eight other friends going with you.

MARK: Yeah. But I hate them. Why does it feel like you don't even care? I don't want to go without you.

CATHY-ANN: Then don't.

MARK: Well, I can't just ditch everyone.

CATHY-ANN: You hate them.

MARK: I don't hate them. It's, like, they're my friends but I can't stand them.

CATHY-ANN: That's never made sense to me.

MARK: It's a gay thing. I dunno. But that's why I really need you there. I feel like shit about myself when I'm around them without you.

CATHY-ANN: Well maybe it's time that we both make some changes.

MARK: So, seriously, you're not coming?

CATHY-ANN: I'm not coming.

MARK: Why do you have to be so fucking serious all the time. It's fucking Pride!

CATHY-ANN: I'm staying home.

MARK: Fine. Bye, boy!

MARK *exits.*

CATHY-ANN: Bye, boy?! That doesn't make any sense coming out of your mouth!

CATHY-ANN *goes back to her laptop and glass of wine.*

Scene 4

NICK: Isn't it "Boy Bye"?

ANDREA: No. *(thinks)* Wait. Maybe you're right?

NICK: I've been saying it wrong for a loooong time. But what do you think of that for the name of the play?

ANDREA: *(thoughtfully, trying it out)* "Boy Bye." "Bye Boy."

NICK: You hate it.

ANDREA: It's just that "Boy Bye" is a dated meme.

NICK: How about "GRRRRRRRL!"?

ANDREA: *(shivers)* Oh God, no!

NICK: What? It works for Black women and gay men.

ANDREA: Can we not use anything that appropriates Black culture, please?

NICK: Well, gay men use that language, too.

ANDREA: Let's not go there. Next.

NICK: Okay. *(deep breath)* How about . . . "He Said/She Said"?

ANDREA: Isn't that a rom-com?

NICK: I love rom-coms!

ANDREA: I know.

NICK: "Glitter Bomb"! "Black and Tan"?

ANDREA: So, can we talk backstory for a little while?

NICK: Gee, I thought you'd never ask.

ANDREA: Do we still think they met in high school?

NICK: I like it better if it was university.

ANDREA: Oh, but I liked it when he was the little gay kid in high school and Cathy-Ann saved him from being picked on. I like the idea that he kind of needed her at first.

NICK: Sure . . .

ANDREA: You don't like it.

NICK: I just like the idea that they met in university. Mark was just coming out and Cathy-Ann was in the same dorm building as him.

ANDREA: Could this possibly be based on your life?

NICK: Maybe a little.

ANDREA: Was your best friend in university Black?

NICK: She was. Did you have gay friends in university?

ANDREA: I had a gay friend in high school! In London, Ontario!

NICK: And were you in love with him?

ANDREA: Oh yeah! Totally a *Love, Simon* storyline.

NICK: Anyways . . . I was thinking that they were both in those hundred-level humanities courses and just like totally became obsessed with HUMAN RIGHTS, and it was those times that young people have when they start putting words to the oppression they've felt and that brings them together. Which is sooo dramatic because then ultimately those social locations are the things that TEAR THEM APART.

ANDREA: You've thought about this a bit.

NICK: I've already written the program notes.

ANDREA: Right.

NICK: Honestly, I'm not a big "backstory" guy. So I can go either way.

ANDREA: But I think it makes a big difference. What kind of experience have they had in the whole gay-white-guy, Black-straight-girl relationship? Did they go to protests together? Or did Mark make Cathy-Ann put him into drag?

NICK: Maybe it's more like Mark and Cathy-Ann used to think that drag was misogynistic and now Mark's making her go to the *RuPaul's Drag Race* tour shows.

ANDREA: And he used to go with her to documentaries and museums but now it's always just gay things.

NICK: Yeah. And like if she ever wanted to go to a straight bar, he'd be like "*eww.*" So I think Mark graduated with a degree in business, which got him some corporate marketing job, and natch he moved right on up the ladder quickly, and then his parents helped him out and he got this two-bedroom condo in the Villy.

ANDREA: Meanwhile, Cathy-Ann finished her degrees and then had to take the first job she could get to start paying off her loans. So she couldn't get out there for real job opportunities and ended up in a whole cycle of contract gigs. Do you think they drifted for a bit?

NICK: Like a year or two? And then reconnected but then suddenly Mark had this big group of gay friends and new clothes and a gym bod. Which I do not have. But if I play the part I will join a gym and get a gym bod. And then write it off in my taxes.

ANDREA: I'll believe it when I see it. They reconnect. It's fun and nostalgic and loving and lots of partying and then she moves in with him.

NICK: Which brings us to the present!

ANDREA: That's it?

NICK: Umm . . . no?

ANDREA: I guess I'm just feeling like . . . who is Cathy-Ann?

NICK: What do you mean?

ANDREA: At the moment, Cathy-Ann feels like a cipher for Mark's character. But who is she off the page?

NICK: Like I said, not a big backstory guy.

ANDREA: I'm really conflicted about this character.

NICK: Why?

ANDREA: She represents a version of who I am, but I don't know how Cathy-Ann squares her race and identity, you know? Who she is? Like, does she have a lot of Black friends, or just acquaintances? She sketches, so does she like to go to the museum and get ideas? We know Mark's dated a bunch—how many boyfriends has she had? Has she ever brought them home? When was the last time she cried? Is she a "hold it in" type? Or "crying at commercials" type?

NICK: Wow. That's so much. How's an actress going to convey all of that in less than ninety minutes?

ANDREA: We'll hire a pro.

NICK: Brilliant. So now what? It's later that night. Mark's been out partying, comes home about 1 a.m. Cathy-Ann is on the couch.

Scene 5

It's 1 a.m. on Pride night, 2016. CATHY-ANN *is sitting in the living room with her laptop, drinking a glass of wine.* MARK *comes home and he's a little tipsy.*

MARK: Hey, girl, heyyyyy!

CATHY-ANN: *(closes laptop hurriedly)* Oh, hey. You're home early.

While speaking MARK *is taking off his shoes and then crosses to get a bottle of water. He checks himself out in the mirror on the way to the couch, then sits. He seems tipsy and a little passive-aggressive.*

MARK: No thanks to you, ho. Everyone split off and I was left all by my lonesome. Well, practically. Mike was with me, but he was on Grindr the whole time. I was all, "*Hey, Mike. We're at a gay bar. This is actually the physical embodiment of Grindr. Just look up.*" And he was all, "*I think I'm going to go to A&W later.*" And I was like, "*Yeah yeah, tell Josh I say hi.*" Anyways. It was fine but it got kinda boring in the end.

CATHY-ANN: You always get like that at the end of Pride. You're partied out.

MARK: Well, my liver is, anyways. I feel like I'm simultaneously drunk and already hungover.

CATHY-ANN: Well, the best cure for that is grease.

CATHY-ANN slides her laptop under a throw pillow and stands up.

What do you want?

MARK: Like, I really want a cheeseburger but feel like I already regret eating it.

CATHY-ANN: Mmm.

MARK: How was your night?

CATHY-ANN: Quiet.

MARK: You loooove your quiet nights.

CATHY-ANN: I do.

There's the sound of a siren going by.

I finally got my sketchbook out again. I can't remember the last—

MARK: I was thinking about you a lot while I was there. Like, the whole time.

CATHY-ANN: Yeah?

MARK: Cathy-Ann, do you remember the sprinkler?

He demonstrates a dance move that they used to do together.

Do you remember it? And it made me think, like, when was the last time we did the sprinkler?

CATHY-ANN: Probably at Ethan's wedding?

MARK: Okay. So last October. Whatever. It made me really miss you. But you were here. At home. You know what we should do? Let's do our annual Meryl marathon. Our Merylathon.

CATHY-ANN: It's 1:15 a.m.

MARK: So? No work tomorrow!

CATHY-ANN: For you. I just want to eat and go to bed.

MARK: Fine, then just one. *Prada*. No. *River Wild*!

MARK picks up CATHY-ANN's laptop.

CATHY-ANN: Can't you use your own laptop?

MARK: It's fucked. Why can't I use yours?

He opens the laptop and looks at it.

What the fuck is this?

CATHY-ANN: It's nothing.

MARK: What the fuck, Cathy-Ann?

CATHY-ANN: Let's just talk about it tomorrow when you're sober.

MARK: Rent-It, Craigslist, House-Hunt . . . You have five tabs of apartment listings open and I'm not supposed to freak out?

CATHY-ANN: You're drunk.

MARK: So, am I imagining this? Oh, look, and you've put in a move-in date for . . . next week?

CATHY-ANN: I was exploring some options.

MARK: And so should I take this as your notice?

CATHY-ANN: Mark, I think we should—

MARK: I let you live here for, like, nothing.

CATHY-ANN: We are not going to have a productive—

MARK: What is happening!? What's your sudden problem with me?

CATHY-ANN: It's not sudden.

MARK: Oh, so you do have a problem with me.

Beat.

CATHY-ANN: You remember my brother. He was pulled over a few weeks ago. You know he's a pastor now? Has his own very loyal congregation, in Ajax, where we never go. So, yeah . . . he gets pulled over because he fits the description.

She shakes her head in disbelief.

And he says, "Sorry, officers, but what's this all about?" They grabbed him and threw him up against the car, yelled at him to calm down. Calm down. Seems like they got the wrong guy. My brother is thirty-one years old, six foot two, and even now could turn you into paste, and when he told me that this had happened to him he cried. He cried so much I felt something inside of me break away. He thought that he'd die that night. And you know, it's not crazy to think that that could happen.

Beat.

MARK: Why didn't you tell me about that?

CATHY-ANN: To be honest, telling you didn't even occur to me.

MARK: Whoa.

CATHY-ANN: Earlier at the parade, security was watching us. I know that because it happens to me all the time. I have experiences that you will never have because I'm Black. Getting asked where I'm from. Being followed in stores. All those videos of Black men shot by police? That could be my brother. Or me. I need you to see me as a Black woman.

MARK: I do!

CATHY-ANN: I don't think you do. And if you won't see me as Black, then you can't see me.

MARK: You're my best friend. Of course I see you!

CATHY-ANN: You see the parts you want to. What happened at the parade today—

MARK: Jesus. It's like you think I'm a monster or something.

CATHY-ANN: That's not what I'm saying.

MARK: Happy fucking Pride!

CATHY-ANN: I am so grateful I went to the parade this year because it was the wake-up call I needed. I'm just so sad that to you Black Lives Matter was a distraction and an offence to your . . . fun.

MARK: You can't just move out with no notice.

CATHY-ANN: I didn't say I was going to. I'm just trying to figure out what I need right now.

MARK: I have done so much for you.

CATHY-ANN: Two-way street.

MARK: It's not fucking fair!

CATHY-ANN: I know.

> *CATHY-ANN storms to her room, MARK to his. Right before exiting, CATHY-ANN stops and turns to MARK. He stops and looks at her. CATHY-ANN turns to the audience.*

I stopped right before going into my room, giving him that one second to—

> *MARK shifts to NICK.*

—that one second to say something, to do something that would—

> *Switch.*

NICK: Andrea?

ANDREA: Sorry, I was just trying something.

NICK: Totally, I just had no idea what was happening.

ANDREA: What if they both had this moment before they go into their bedrooms where they turn and glance at each other— But then they both go into this internal monologue, direct address moment about what's going on in their heads.

NICK: . . . Okay.

ANDREA: No?

NICK: Just . . . I wonder if it's jarring. Like sudden direct address.

ANDREA: We already used the convention earlier, at the Pride parade.

NICK: True . . .

ANDREA: It would be weird if we didn't use it again.

NICK: Yeah, totally. Or maybe we cut *that* scene?

ANDREA: Really?

NICK: I dunno . . .

ANDREA: We've already done it at like four fundraisers.

NICK: Yeah, and I like the Ganglezar bit.

ANDREA: So then they look at each other at the bedroom door, then turn out—

NICK: I just don't think it's here.

ANDREA: Okay.

NICK: We already have that big monologue, and then another—

ANDREA: Yeah.

NICK: Can we just try it for now, that they just look at each other then go into their rooms.

ANDREA: Sure.

NICK: Cool. Are you sure?

ANDREA: Totally.

Switch.

NICK: It's not fucking fair!

CATHY-ANN: I know.

They storm up stage to their bedroom doors, then turn and look at one another. They hold a long stare at each other, then exit to their rooms.

Scene 6

NICK and ANDREA re-enter.

ANDREA: I think we have a problem.

NICK: We do?

ANDREA: Everyone is going to ask, why are Mark and Cathy-Ann friends?

NICK: Yeah.

ANDREA: Yup.

NICK: But we know. It's that thing. That way that friendships start in one place and slowly, painfully can turn totally toxic, but it takes a long time to—

ANDREA: I know. I know that and you know that.

NICK: So . . .

ANDREA: I think I'm getting stuck writing this play because Mark has been written as intractable and irredeemable.

NICK: I don't even know what one of those words means.

ANDREA: I mean—okay, I get that you're drawing from real guys you've met and talked to about this BLM Pride issue, and thank goodness for that, since I don't know anyone so hostile to the events that day.

NICK: I'm kind of toning him down, actually.

ANDREA: I get that. Sometimes that nasty element doesn't always serve the piece. It just seems to exist as an opportunity to pile on and make an audience feel superior.

NICK: I see.

ANDREA: I can write a great fight, but once after a reading of one of my plays the dramaturg said "good conflict, but where is the love?"

NICK: Fuck that guy!

ANDREA: Remember in acting school we're told not to judge the characters we're playing?

NICK: You think I'm judging Mark? This guy exists.

ANDREA: Mark is almost a cartoon bad guy in this narrative and, even though we haven't been writing it in, I really think he has some sweet, lovable qualities that we're not seeing. Why has Cathy-Ann loved him all these years?

NICK: Because of what they had in the past.

ANDREA: Right, but Cathy-Ann isn't an idiot.

NICK: I never said that she was an idiot.

ANDREA: And yet you have her being friends with a total asshole.

NICK: *Now* who's judging him?

ANDREA: That's not what I mean.

NICK: I know what you mean. I think that the thing about Mark is that he's charismatic and that's why people like him, but actually he's a really like intolerant guy.

ANDREA: Are you worried that people will think that Mark is you?

NICK: *(slowly)* Am I worried people are going to think that Mark is me?

ANDREA: Every time we have this conversation you seem to agree that functionally we need to believe that Mark and Cathy-Ann would be friends, but then in your next draft he does or says something even more unlikeable.

NICK: Gee, thanks.

ANDREA: It's not a criticism of your writing. Or no, I guess it is. It needs to be. Because it's our biggest hurdle in the play. If there's no argument for their relationship, for *Mark*, then this play has no juice or edge or anything.

NICK: So what do you suggest?

ANDREA: Some sort of scene earlier that makes Mark more likeable.

NICK: Okay. Go nuts.

ANDREA: Let's go back. Maybe it's during the scene in the apartment after the parade. Cathy-Ann and Mark are snuggling on the sofa. It's cozy.

Switch.

MARK: You know, as we got closer to College Street, during the parade, I got really scared.

CATHY-ANN: Why?

MARK: I thought something bad was about to happen. Like, I got this cold, tense feeling in my stomach.

CATHY-ANN: I know that one. Like when you know you're going to get dumped.

MARK: Or jumped by a gang of homophobic assholes who yell faggot at you.

CATHY-ANN: Oh, Mark.

MARK: It's fine. It's only happened a couple of times, and I always outran them.

CATHY-ANN: Still . . .

MARK: That gang of people from a distance looked threatening. Dressed in black, some on the ground. Scary. I was sure something violent was going to go down.

CATHY-ANN: Yeah, but then—

MARK: That woman with the megaphone was terrifying.

CATHY-ANN: Terrifying? Nooooo.

MARK: She looked like a man.

CATHY-ANN: *(stiffening)* No, she didn't.

MARK: She was built like Serena Williams, you know? Just jacked. I would not want to meet her in a dark alley.

CATHY-ANN pulls herself up off the sofa, letting MARK fall backwards.

CATHY-ANN: You can't say that Black women look like men!

MARK: Some of them do.

CATHY-ANN: What you're saying is an affront to Black women, and I am a Black woman!

MARK: And you're adorbs. Don't be mad.

CATHY-ANN: I'm not mad, I'm . . . I'm disappointed that you just don't get it.

CATHY-ANN exits.

Switch.

NICK: That's your scene that's supposed to make Mark more likeable?

ANDREA: I think it's based in feelings instead of brains, which is more relatable.

NICK: I think that someone would throw something at Mark's head.

ANDREA: It was a first draft.

NICK: I'm not feeling it. And that's not because I'm worried people will think I'm racist.

ANDREA: Oh my God.

NICK: Okay, let me try something—I don't know where this would go . . .

Switch.

CATHY-ANN: Where do you see us in five years?

MARK: I don't know. Why don't you tell me what you think?

CATHY-ANN: Well, I see myself as working in a permanent, full-time job, living on my own, being in a relationship, and hopefully being very, very settled. But you, Mark, I see you being sad.

MARK: Excuse me?

CATHY-ANN: You party four nights a week. You use cocaine and drink way too much. And all of this sex. What are you running from?

Switch.

ANDREA: *(laughing)* Oh my God! Mark does cocaine?! Now *I'm* sad.

NICK: You hate it.

ANDREA: No, I'm just . . . I really didn't think it would get so dark.

NICK: Shit's getting real.

ANDREA: Damn . . . Blow.

Switch.

CATHY-ANN: You party four nights a week. You use cocaine and drink way too much. And all of this sex. What are you running from?

MARK: I'm not running from anything.

CATHY-ANN: I know that it's all an act that you learned growing up with a relationship that was way too bonded with your mother and afraid of your father's rejection. You overcompensate to please Momma by getting the good job, living in the nice condo, bleaching your teeth, and doing squats. But there's a price to pay for that. And like other gays, that gap is filled by doing drugs, partying too much, treating each other like shit, being racist, and having dangerous, unloving sex with multiple partners, all in the guise of sexual liberation.

MARK: Go to Hell, Cathy-Ann.

CATHY-ANN: See you there.

MARK storms off.

Switch.

NICK looks at ANDREA expectantly.

ANDREA: What was that?

NICK: Maybe Cathy-Ann's homophobic. Like *really* homophobic, not just a prude.

ANDREA: Well.

NICK: That could even out the conflict a bit, couldn't it? Muddy the waters?

ANDREA: Not really.

NICK: Why? Why wouldn't that work?

ANDREA: Making both of them intolerable—

NICK: I think it makes her more human.

ANDREA: Not really.

NICK: Are you worried that people might think that you're homophobic?

ANDREA: No. That's not it at all.

NICK: No?

ANDREA: Really. No. Not even a tiny bit.

NICK: Why? Why's it different than what you asked me?

ANDREA: Because no one who sees me in this play is going to believe that I, Andrea, am homophobic.

NICK: But they're going to think that I, Nick, am racist?

ANDREA: I didn't say that.

NICK: But you asked if I worry about it.

ANDREA: It was a question because you actually voiced that worry in the playwright's unit.

NICK: Okay.

ANDREA: I was just saying that we need to make Mark more likeable, so that it's more of a—

NICK: I get it! I agree with you! I get it and I agree with you!

ANDREA: Jesus, it wasn't a personal attack, Nick!

NICK: I know! You just seem so angry about it for some reason.

ANDREA: Really? Really?

NICK: Or not angry. I just mean . . . it felt a little personal when you asked me that out of the blue.

ANDREA: Not an attack.

NICK: Okay. Fine. Can we just keep working, please?

ANDREA: I thought we *were* working.

NICK: I think we should pick it up three days later, in the morning.

ANDREA: All right.

NICK: And hopefully I'll be— *Mark* will be more likeable, or—

ANDREA: It's the morning?

NICK: Three days later. Mark and Cathy-Ann haven't spoken in a few days.

CATHY-ANN has found a place to live and has started to pack. It's the morning and she's getting some orange juice from the fridge; it is tense.

Scene 7

CATHY-ANN opens the fridge, pulls out a carton of orange juice, pours a glass, and drinks it while standing at the counter. She goes to the cupboard to get a box of cereal but there's none there. She goes to the pantry cupboard, opens it, and there's the box on the top shelf. Too high for her to grab. MARK has walked out of his room and sees her staring up at the cereal, so he reaches up to get it for her.

CATHY-ANN: Thanks.

MARK: No problem.

MARK opens the fridge, hands CATHY-ANN the milk, and drinks the orange juice from the carton. CATHY-ANN sits at the kitchen table and eats her cereal.

Booked your mover yet?

CATHY-ANN: Uh . . . no . . . My parents are going to help me.

MARK: Hm.

Beat.

I think I'm going to take a trip.

CATHY-ANN: Yeah?

MARK: I was thinking—

CATHY-ANN: Are we talking now?

MARK: Thought I'd give it a try. If you're up to it.

CATHY-ANN: Okay . . .

MARK: I've kind of run out of silence.

CATHY-ANN: Yeah, me too.

MARK: Yeah.

CATHY-ANN: What were you saying?

MARK: Just that I was thinking I'd go travelling.

CATHY-ANN: Where?

MARK: I don't know yet. I've been looking at Instagram. Places like Cabo, London, Vietnam . . . so far from here.

CATHY-ANN: Vietnam would be nice.

MARK: It'd be nice to get a break from all the bullshit here. Do something that really matters.

CATHY-ANN: You can get the time off work?

MARK: Oh I'm sure they can find someone else who can write some stupid corporate tweets for a couple weeks. Though they won't have my flair.

CATHY-ANN: Obviously.

MARK: Remember when we kinda sorta talked about going to Scotland?

CATHY-ANN: You wanted to get an authentic traditional kilt for the MacDonald clan.

MARK: And you wanted to see if there were any actual Black Scotsmen. But we didn't make it.

CATHY-ANN: Because *(shrugs)* life happens.

MARK: You can say it.

CATHY-ANN *shakes her head.*

People die.

CATHY-ANN: I really loved your mom, Mark. She was so kind to me.

MARK: She always wanted a daughter. And you're so girly she wished you were around all the time.

CATHY-ANN: That's so sweet. She was so generous with me. She gave me this sweater!

MARK: I'd say to her, "I'll wear a dress if it'll make you happy, Mom." I was, like, eight when I said it to her as she lingered over the section in the clothing catalogue for girls. And she said—I'll never forget her tone—she said, "No no no, Markie, boys don't wear skirts and dresses. You'll grow up big and strong and play football with your brothers." She said it like she was willing it into being. She knew that I was gay but pretended that she didn't. She wanted you to be my girlfriend.

CATHY-ANN: Mark.

MARK: Sometimes I'd say something at dinner and it would come out so gay, like a handbag would fall out of my mouth, *that* gay. And she'd get this grim, pained look on her face. Kind of like the one you have now.

CATHY-ANN: I just wish you weren't so hard on yourself.

MARK: I'm not being hard on myself. I love myself and my femmy femmy voice. I do. I love it and it's part of my identity. It always has been. The other day at brunch someone was giving me side-eye for being all like, "*Hey, girl. What's up, girl,*" and I was like, you know what? That's what I sound like. Like, me not talking like that is actually the affectation. I don't know if my mom ever accepted that before she died.

Beat.

So, where are you moving to?

CATHY-ANN: The east end.

MARK: Ohhh.

CATHY-ANN: Yeah, it's going to be like discovering a whole new part of the city.

MARK: Is it a nice building?

CATHY-ANN: It's a house.

MARK: Oh.

CATHY-ANN: It has a big backyard, and a barbecue. There's even a clothesline to dry my clothes.

MARK: Sounds very domestic.

CATHY-ANN: *(smiles stiffly)* It'll be nice living around a lot of trees and away from the crazy traffic.

MARK: Take longer to get to work.

CATHY-ANN: I'll be driving in. With my roommate.

MARK: Who— . . . What?

CATHY-ANN: I'm moving in with Teresa.

MARK: Teresa?

CATHY-ANN: Yeah.

MARK: You hate her.

CATHY-ANN: No, I don't. She's gotten on my nerves, but I don't hate her. We eat lunch together all the time.

MARK: So, you're moving in . . . with a co-worker?

CATHY-ANN: She actually lives on another floor of the house. But yes.

MARK: Oh.

CATHY-ANN: The timing is excellent. She just renovated her basement into a beautiful apartment and was leery about living with a stranger.

MARK: And you're not a stranger?

CATHY-ANN: I'm not. This is good. Just like you wanting to travel and stuff, this allows me to get out of my comfort zone a little.

MARK: Right.

It gets quiet for a bit.

Teresa's Black.

CATHY-ANN: And?

MARK: Uh-huh.

CATHY-ANN: What?

MARK: Nothing. It's just interesting that you'd leave me to live with a Black woman.

CATHY-ANN: What does her being Black have to do with anything?

MARK: It just feels pointed. Deliberate.

CATHY-ANN: This is not about you! I'm excited to live with someone who understands some of the experiences that I just can't talk to you about.

MARK: You mean what a drag it was to live with your racist white homo friend?

CATHY-ANN: Oh my GAAAWWD!! I was thinking that it would be amazing to talk to her about hair, and good places to get roti, and, shit,

I dunno, Black women stuff. But please continue to think that every move I make has everything to do with you.

CATHY-ANN crosses to the door, then stops and looks over at MARK. She then turns out to the audience.

I stopped by the door, looking at him . . . basically begging him to say something—

Switch.

NICK: Are we doing it here then?

ANDREA: Can you just try it?

NICK: 'Kay.

Switch.

CATHY-ANN: —begging him to say something.

MARK: She's standing there, staring. What am I supposed to say?

CATHY-ANN: But what. What could he say?

MARK: I can't believe she's moving out tomorrow. There are no words.

CATHY-ANN: Silence. The corrosive silence that has led to so much pain and distance between us. Silence that's like—

Switch.

NICK: Sorry. Sorry, Andrea, I'm really not feeling this here.

ANDREA: Oh. Okay.

NICK: Can we just take a sec? Take a step back?

ANDREA: Sure.

Scene 8

NICK writes on his flip chart paper as he speaks:

NICK: Okay, let's just talk about this structurally.

ANDREA: Okay.

NICK: Scene 1 we have before the parade—

He writes on a Post-it Note and sticks it to the set.

ANDREA: The scene in the condo.

NICK: Getting ready, fun and frivolity.

ANDREA: Cathy-Ann is dressed like a sentient rainbow.

NICK: Exactly. Okay. Scene 2 is at the parade.

ANDREA: Let's do our two characters "at work."

She writes on a Post-it.

NICK: Okay. And that's . . . ?

ANDREA: Like intercut monologues or two big, long back-to-back monologues. I want to work in a story about this friend of mine who is this big Trump supporter.

NICK: I am totally happy to try anything you want to try.

ANDREA: Okay, so. At work.

NICK: All right. And then how about Scene 3 is "After the Parade."

He writes on a Post-it.

ANDREA: I'd like to see how they met.

NICK: Okay . . .

ANDREA: What if we went the parade, then them meeting in high school?

She writes "High School" on a Post-it and sticks it next to the first one.

NICK: Did we agree on them meeting in high school or university?

ANDREA: Well now there's that monologue about the brother, who Mark knew in high school.

NICK: Yeah. If we keep that.

ANDREA: Oh.

NICK: We don't have to decide now.

ANDREA: Okay. What happens next?

NICK: After the parade. "Well you don't see me sitting down at Caribana." "No, Mark, you'd have to actually come to Caribana for that to happen."

ANDREA: That's so good.

NICK: And then Mark storms out and . . . boom.

He writes on a Post-it.

"1 a.m. Chat." Craigslist? House-Hunt?!

ANDREA: Ouch.

NICK: It's not pretty.

ANDREA: What if . . . what if before, we went: "University Days."

She writes the Post-it, then goes and replaces the "1 a.m. Chat" one with it.

Monologues from when they were forming their identity.

NICK: 'Kay.

ANDREA: You know, like how Mark and Cathy-Ann were really politically engaged when they started their friendship. They were doing all of these equity studies classes and gender studies.

NICK: So like the Judith Butler years?

ANDREA: Yeah. You could do a monologue on that pineapple theory thing you wrote.

NICK: That was the worst thing I have ever written.

ANDREA: It was the worst thing you have ever written.

NICK: Okay, so you want to do another flashback thing here.

ANDREA: Well if you want to.

NICK: Sure. Sure. I am up for trying anything.

ANDREA: You've mentioned that.

NICK: Flashback. "1 a.m. Chat." SHE'S MOVING OUT, OMG, WHAT A BITCH. Next scene . . . "Packing, Three Days Later."

He writes the Post-it and goes to place it in line.

ANDREA: Sorry . . .

NICK: No, no that's fine.

He makes a U-turn and puts the Post-it back on the stand.

ANDREA: I love this image of the lights going down on Cathy-Ann with the laptop glow on her face. What if, instead . . .

She starts to write on her Post-it.

. . . it went to Cathy-Ann and Mark at work. Cathy-Ann tired of the bullshit in the job that she is totally overqualified for. Mark relishing in the power position that he's in.

NICK: Okay. And so struuuuuucturally . . .

ANDREA: I think it gives a glimpse into the price Mark has to pay to have the privilege that's now tearing him and Cathy-Ann apart.

NICK: So this would be part of the flashback arc?

ANDREA: Sure. You could look at this that way.

NICK: Okay, so it's "1 a.m. Chat," "Work Life," then "Packing, Three Days Later." Which leads to . . . Andrea, are you ready for it?

ANDREA: Flashback?

NICK: No! I was thinking we could have a monologue here. Something from Cathy-Ann.

ANDREA: Okay, how about something with her parents? I was thinking that she maybe lied to them about living with a gay guy.

NICK: Yeah, that's great.

He writes "Monologue, Cathy-Ann" on a Post-it, then places it next to "Packing, Three Days Later."

ANDREA: Or . . . what if they both broke into a scene with their parents.

NICK: So . . . a flashback.

ANDREA: Well—

She writes as she talks.

—a flashback monologue.

She sticks the Post-it "Flashback Monologue—Parents" next to "Packing, Three Days Later."

NICK: Yeah. Okay, so they meet up while packing, flashback to parents, and then boom . . . back to the present where we get to "The Big Fight." It blows away any hope for resolution.

ANDREA: I love that.

NICK: They both storm off in tears.

ANDREA: Can you get tears out?

NICK: If I don't sleep the night before. So then we go on next to the last scene.

ANDREA: What if now we go back again to when they first met?

NICK: So you want two more scenes at the end?

ANDREA: I think it would be powerful to go back to that first day they met. Then to "Moving Day." Like "hello" to "goodbye."

NICK: Okay. Put that up there.

> ANDREA *puts up a Post-it that says "High School Two," then* NICK *puts the Post-it up for "Moving Day."*

There it is.

ANDREA: There it is. Okay, see you at opening.

NICK: Very funny. I'm just . . .

ANDREA: Yes? ·

NICK: Don't kill me, but I'm not sure about it.

ANDREA: Okay.

NICK: Let's just look at this structurally for a minute.

ANDREA: Sure.

NICK: Okay, so we have "Before the Parade"—happy happy fun times. It's the status quo. Then they go off to the parade. Inciting incident, and then from there . . . I think they need to return home. I'm worried this flashback would take away too much from our big inciting incident.

ANDREA: Take it down.

He takes off "High School."

NICK: I'm just trying something. You don't mind, right?

ANDREA: Not at all.

NICK: Okay, so we see the status quo, we see the moment that changes everything irrevocably. I think from here the central conflict is Mark's resistance to change versus Cathy-Ann's growing understanding of what needs to happen, and it's about hoping that they can reconcile. And that's where the climax lies, so we have to build there. Obstacle one: big fight after the parade, off Mark goes. Then . . . sorry—

He takes off "University Days."

—then he comes home, it's 1 a.m. He missed her at the club. He looks on the laptop and sees that she has been apartment hunting. Oh shit, what a bitch. Obstacle two. Cathy-Ann gets a huge monologue about her brother. He storms off, and then . . . I'm so sorry, just bear with me . . .

He removes the "At Work" monologues Post-it.

It's three days later, she's packing. They have a moment of tenderness, we think, OMG, THEY'RE GOING TO MAKE UP! And then, boom, Mark says something really dumb, something showing that truly the incident at the parade has shifted everything and their relationship can't go on as it did before—CLIMAX OF THE PLAY. Both exit in a huff. And from here . . .

He takes down "High School Two."

We go to the falling action and resolution. Moving day, boxes are taken out. We will collaborate on a beautiful scene in which they reflect on their relationship. Make peace. Say goodbye. Something sad, something hopeful. In the end, Mark remains alone on stage, in his condo; the place that was bought with the privilege that now leaves him alone. There. The end.

> *Throughout,* ANDREA *has taken the Post-its that* NICK *has removed and placed them on her body.*

And so, do you see what this is?

ANDREA: *The Glass Menagerie?*

NICK: What? No. We have the given circumstances, inciting incident, rising action with obstacles, climax, then falling action and resolution.

ANDREA: Yeah?

NICK: Yeah? I mean I think so?

ANDREA: Because it looks like a linear play in almost real time set in a white guy's living room.

NICK: Well, no, there's the scene at the parade.

ANDREA: Right.

NICK: You don't like it . . .

ANDREA: It's just that I've seen it. Over and over. A million times.

NICK: I'm not so— Just because it's set in a living room?

ANDREA: Maybe we should take a break.

NICK: Yeah?

ANDREA: Why are we writing this play?

NICK: I think it's an important moment that we should be—

ANDREA: Yes, I read your section of the grant proposal. But, actually, why are you writing it?

NICK: Well, *we* are writing it.

ANDREA: Sure, but it was your idea first. You came to me with it.

NICK: Well besides the fact that I think you're brilliant and want to work with you?

ANDREA: Yes, but that's obvious, who wouldn't want to work with me? But actually.

NICK: I think I was thinking that this is something new, something Toronto. Something very us.

ANDREA: Yes, yes, no that's not what I'm asking. I know the political intentions.

NICK: I'm not sure what you're asking.

ANDREA: What are you, Nick, wanting to say about yourself as an artist by writing this play?

NICK: I'm hoping that you and I, together, can tackle some issues in coalition. It's about coalition. The possibilities of using art to—

ANDREA: That's the grant proposal. I'm asking *you*.

NICK: It feels like you're implying that I have ulterior motives.

ANDREA: Which are?

NICK: I don't *have* ulterior motives.

ANDREA: I'm not saying that you do.

NICK: So why are you writing this play?

ANDREA: I guess I want to see what happens.

NICK: Oh, how noble.

ANDREA: What does that mean?

NICK: Nothing. That's why I'm writing it too. To see what happens.

ANDREA: Okay.

NICK: Okay.

    Beat.

Do we need to talk about something?

ANDREA: You keep backing away from the real question.

NICK: I think that I face them right on. In fact, I think that you come out a lot better than I do in all of this.

ANDREA: You mean Cathy-Ann comes out a lot better.

NICK: Yes.

ANDREA: Exactly.

NICK: Exactly what?

ANDREA: And Mark's *not you.*

NICK: And?

ANDREA: So you're not so awful, like other gay white guys out there.

NICK: And there it is.

ANDREA: What?

NICK: My ulterior motives that you think I have.

ANDREA: Well. Have you ever thought maybe that's why you wanted to write this?

NICK: Jesus.

ANDREA: You're able to write about an incident that is about racism, but you can come off without any blood on your hands.

NICK: That was not my intention, Andrea.

ANDREA: We're in a time when racialized stories are being prioritized, and you're able to be a part of that conversation by condemning your own community. You can get the grant money and still be white.

NICK: Believe it or not, I didn't propose this idea for the whopping thousand dollars in grant money. I think that this could be an important piece of theatre if we write it together.

ANDREA: But why do you think that it has to be told together?

NICK: Because it was my idea.

ANDREA: So then why wouldn't you write it yourself?

NICK: You know the answer to that question.

ANDREA: Why can't you say it?

NICK: Because that wasn't my motive when I asked you.

ANDREA: So then why did you ask me, Nick?

NICK: Honestly, right now? I have no idea.

ANDREA: That's what I thought.

NICK: I didn't mean that.

ANDREA: I know you didn't. But I hope you keep thinking about it.

Scene 9

July 8, 2016. CATHY-ANN *tapes up another box.* MARK *stands and watches her. She picks up the box and goes to put it with the others behind where* MARK *is standing. He doesn't move.*

CATHY-ANN: Can you move, please?

MARK moves out of the way. He goes and leans against the wall, watching her pack. CATHY-ANN *continues to pack in silence, glancing at him a few times.*

Are you just going to stand there and watch?

MARK: Would you rather I left?

CATHY-ANN: Do whatever you want. It's your place, right?

MARK: Right.

CATHY-ANN: Right.

There's another beat of CATHY-ANN *packing and* MARK *watching.*

MARK: *(brightly)* So, I guess we're finally out of things to talk about.

CATHY-ANN: Don't do that.

MARK: What?

CATHY-ANN: Make a joke.

MARK: Who's joking?

CATHY-ANN: You've made the last few days hell. You're not going to alleviate your guilt by trying to pretend like you're the nice guy here.

MARK: Wow. Are you psychologizing me right now? Is that what's happening?

CATHY-ANN: I'm just saying it like it is.

MARK: I'm so glad. I'm so glad you're able to finally say it like it is. Because, *apparently*, you've been sitting on your total hatred of me for the last million years of us being friends.

CATHY-ANN: If that's your interpretation of what's happening here, then we have really, officially run out of things to say to each other.

MARK: I guess you're right.

Silence.

You know, it's not like I didn't know that things have been changing for us.

CATHY-ANN: I know that. You've told me how lame I am now, compared to when I used to buzz around behind you.

MARK: That's not—I thought we were changing together. You're a big part of *who* I've become. Like, don't you feel that? At least a little bit?

CATHY-ANN: If I've been a part of who you are today, then I feel like I've failed you.

MARK: Oh.

CATHY-ANN: Honestly, Mark? I guess I've realized that there are parts of me that can't exist in this relationship because I see the world differently than I did when I met you.

MARK: So, it's all my fault.

CATHY-ANN: You can't step into the same river twice. People change. We've changed.

MARK: Whatever.

CATHY-ANN: *(sigh)* You asked.

MARK: I'm gonna go. When's your dad coming?

CATHY-ANN: In an hour.

MARK: Fine. Just put the keys under the mat.

CATHY-ANN: I will.

MARK: Okay. Um. Bye.

CATHY-ANN: Bye.

MARK: Bye.

> *MARK begins to leave.*

CATHY-ANN: I did love you. Still kinda do.

MARK: Right.

> *MARK crosses to the door. He turns and looks over at CATHY-ANN. There is a long silence as they stare at each other, then MARK turns out to the audience:*

She has this look in her eye. It's hard, like the door's already closed.

CATHY-ANN: It won't work.

MARK: It's so quiet. I take a breath—

CATHY-ANN: It's not—

MARK: —go to say that one thing, that one thing that will—

CATHY-ANN: It's too late.

    Beat.

MARK: It's too late.

    MARK exits. CATHY-ANN is alone on stage. The lights go to black.

Scene 10

NICK and ANDREA stand in the darkness.

NICK: Do you think that's the end?

ANDREA: I don't know. It's dark.

NICK: In more ways than one.

NICK opens his laptop, his face illuminated by it.

It doesn't seem right that she just moves out at the end. They fight and she leaves and, what? They never talk again?

ANDREA: The way things stand now? Yes.

NICK: I don't think I'm happy with that.

ANDREA opens her laptop.

ANDREA: I don't think I'm happy with a bit more than that.

NICK: Like the writing?

ANDREA: No. Yes and no.

NICK: Can we fix it?

ANDREA: Maybe.

NICK: Like what if Mark apologizes or something?

ANDREA: I don't think it's a small rewrite.

NICK: Right.

ANDREA: We'd probably have to start over.

NICK: From the beginning?

ANDREA: Well, either that or just give the fuck up.

NICK: Maybe. We'd have to return the thousand dollars.

A weak laugh. Pause.

This is really hard work.

ANDREA: Try living it.

NICK: How does anyone do it?

ANDREA: Every day you rise.

NICK: That's it, eh?

ANDREA: That's it.

Beat.

NICK: What do you want to do?

ANDREA: I don't know. What do you want to do?

NICK: I don't know. I'm pretty tired.

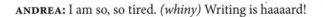

ANDREA: I am so, so tired. *(whiny)* Writing is haaaard!

NICK: Yeah.

They look at each other in the glow of the laptops, then back at their screens.

Wanna go for martinis?

ANDREA: And you're buying.

They smile at each other.

NICK: Fuck yeah!

Switch!

The laptops snap shut.

The end.

Andrea Scott's play *Eating Pomegranates Naked* won the RBC Arts Professional Award and was named Outstanding Production at the 2013 SummerWorks Festival. *Better Angels: A Parable* won the SummerWorks Award for Outstanding Production. Both were published by Scirocco Drama in 2018. *Don't Talk to Me Like I'm Your Wife,* which won the Cayle Chernin Award for theatre, ran at SummerWorks in 2016. 2019 saw her co-written play with Nick Green, *Every Day She Rose* wow audiences at Buddies in Bad Times Theatre. Her play about Viola Desmond, *Controlled Damage,* had its sold-out world premiere at Neptune Theatre in 2020 and won four Robert Merritt Awards. It will open at the Grand Theatre in their 2022/2023 season. She won the Magee Diversity Screenwriter's Award for her first TV script, *Dust to Dust.* Her dark comedy *Bad Habits* landed her a job in the all-Black writer's room of *The Porter* (BET/CBC), which she followed up by snagging a spot pitching her supernatural drama *Cassidy Must Die* to Netflix. 2021 saw her winning $10,000 from Amazon and the Indigenous Screen Office, pitching her coming-of-age dramedy *DONE!* She's currently working in the writer's room on the sixteenth season of *Murdoch Mysteries.*

Nick Green is a Dora and Sterling Award–winning playwright, and the creator of the Social Distancing Festival. Credits include *Happy Birthday Baby J* (Shadow Theatre); *Every Day She Rose* (Nightwood Theatre, co-written with Andrea Scott); *Fangirl* (book; Launch Pad at the Musical Stage Company); *In Real Life* (book; Canadian Music Theatre Projects); *Dinner with the Duchess* (Next Stage Festival, BroadwayWorld Toronto Award); *Body Politic* (Buddies in Bad Times/lemonTree Creations; Dora Award); *Poof! The Musical* (book and lyrics; Capitol Theatre, Sterling Award nomination); and *The Fabulous Buddha Boi* (Guys UnDisguised, Sterling Award). He lives in Toronto.